Yes, HE CARES

by

WOODROW KROLL

YES, HE CARES
published by Back to the Bible
©1998 by Woodrow Kroll

International Standard Book Number
0-8474-0687-3

Edited by Rachel Derowitsch
Cover concept by Laura Goodspeed

Unless otherwise noted, all Scripture is taken from *The New King James Version.*
Copyright © 1979, 1980, 1982,
Thomas Nelson, Inc.
Used by permission.

ALL RIGHTS RESERVED
No part of this publication may be reproduced, stored in a retrieval system or transmitted, in any form or by any means—electronic, mechanical photocopying, recording or otherwise—except for brief quotations in printed reviews or articles, without the prior written permission of the publisher.

For information:
BACK TO THE BIBLE
POST OFFICE BOX 82808
LINCOLN, NEBRASKA 68501
1 2 3 4 5 6 7 8 9—04 03 02 01 00 99 98

Printed in the USA

CONTENTS

The Compassionate Heart of Jesus	5
Does Jesus Care When I'm Burdened?	17
Does Jesus Care When I Worry?	31
Does Jesus Care When I've Failed?	43
Does Jesus Care When I Sorrow?	55
Oh, Yes, He Cares!	65

CHAPTER ONE

The Compassionate Heart of Jesus

Have you ever felt as if you were abandoned? Do you think you've been left alone to struggle with your trials and difficulties? Many of us have.

In 1901, Reverend Frank Graeff was struggling with feelings just like this. He went through such a deep and heartbreaking personal experience that later he observed his "whole attitude had become one of despair and defeat." Each day seemed to find him slipping deeper and deeper into depression and despondency.

Finally, Frank Graeff dropped to his knees and poured out his heart to God. Then God led him to 1 Peter 5:7, which says, "casting all your care upon Him, for He cares for you." As the discouraged pastor meditated on that verse, God brought afresh the assurance that He did care. Frank felt an uncanny joy flood his soul and shortly thereafter penned this hymn:

Does Jesus care when my heart is pained too deeply for mirth and song;
As the burdens press, and the cares distress, and the way grows weary and long?
Does Jesus care when my way is dark with

a nameless dread and fear?

As the daylight fades into deep night shades, does He care enough to be near?

Does Jesus care when I've tried and failed to resist some temptation strong;

When for my deep grief I find no relief, though my tears flow all the night long?

Does Jesus care when I've said good-by to the dearest on earth to me,

And my sad heart aches till it nearly breaks—is it aught to Him? Does He see?

To each of these questions the encouraged pastor responded:

Oh, yes, He cares; I know He cares!

His heart is touched with my grief;

When the days are weary, the long nights dreary, I know my Saviour cares.

As Reverend Graeff discovered, the essence of Jesus is a compassionate heart. Jesus loves you. He really loves you. He has a marvelously compassionate heart. But what does that mean? What is genuine compassion? If you're feeling alone in your struggles in life, what does Jesus' compassion mean to you?

Compassion is more than pity

There is more to genuine compassion than just pity for those around us. Pity is not wrong; it is a noble emotion. We often pity others in unfortunate circumstances. But we haven't had compassion on them.

The Bible contains many stories of people who have had pity on others. Exodus 2 describes the tender story of the baby Moses placed in a basket and left in the bulrushes. When the daughter of Pharaoh came to the river for her early morning bath, she saw the basket among the reeds and sent one of her maids to bring it to her. Exodus 2:6 says, "And when she had opened it, she saw the child, and behold, the baby wept. So she 'had compassion on him, and said, "This is one of the Hebrews' children."'" The word translated as "compassion" in this verse is the Hebrew word *chamal*. Literally, it means "to take mercy on" or "to be pitiful about."

This same word is used in 1 Samuel 23. On one occasion, as Saul pursued David, the Ziphites tipped off Saul as to where David's hideout was. Verse 21 records Saul's words: "Blessed are you of the LORD, for you have compassion on me." This doesn't mean that the Ziphites loved Saul; it simply means that they had pity (*chamal*) on him. They felt sorry for him. *Pity* is a better word choice for the emotions here.

Compassion is much more difficult than pity. Theologian Henri Nouwen observed, "Let us not underestimate how hard it is to be compassionate. Compassion is hard because it requires the inner disposition to go with others to the place where they are weak, vulnerable, lonely and broken. But this is not our spontaneous response to suffering. What we desire most is to do away with suffering by fleeing from it or finding a quick cure for it."

Nouwen is right. It isn't easy to be compassionate. In fact, Erwin Lutzer says, "Christianity demands a level of caring that transcends human inclinations." Your inclination and mine, when we see a person in need, is to have pity on that person and respond with a quick fix. Compassion, on the other hand, is selfless love that is willing to be involved on a long-term basis.

Unlike the Ziphites, unlike Pharaoh's daughter and unlike, sometimes, you and me, God does not simply pity us; He has compassion on us. The New International Version of the Bible translates Psalm 78:38 as, "Yet he [God] was merciful; he forgave their iniquities and did not destroy them." But *merciful* is not a strong enough word here. The word used in this verse means "to love deeply" or "to have tender affection for." The reason God would not destroy Israel is because He had a deep and tender love for them. He was compassionate toward them. He was not just full of pity; He was full of compassion. Psalm 86:15 says, "But You, O Lord, are a compassionate and gracious God, slow to anger, abounding in love and faithfulness" (NIV).

Pity means that you look at a person and you feel badly for him. Compassion means that you look at that same person and you love him. Pity hands a dollar to a homeless person; compassion find a shelter for him.

Compassion is based on commitment

Compassion may be accompanied by feelings, but it is more than a feeling. Compassion is a commitment. We may have a feeling of pity or a feeling of love, but the problem with feelings is that they come and go. People enter and leave relationships because their feelings change. But real compassion continues on (sometimes in spite of our feelings) because it's based on a committed relationship.

Second Kings 13:23 describes God's attitude toward Israel. "The LORD was gracious to them, had compassion on them, and regarded them, because of His covenant with Abraham, Isaac, and Jacob, and would not yet destroy them or cast them from His presence." This verse shows that God doesn't simply feel kindly toward Israel; He has made a commitment to them. It is a commitment based on the covenants He made with Abraham, Isaac and Jacob.

In the same way, God shows compassion to you and me. Lamentations 3:32 says, "Though He causes grief, yet He will show compassion according to the multitude of His mercies." God has a commitment to us. He is committed to our welfare. He is committed to our salvation. He is committed to our future. After all, He gave His Son to die for us. That's the deepest commitment you'll ever know. God doesn't show compassion on us just because He likes us. He shows compassion on us because He is committed to us.

Compassion flows out of character

Furthermore, while pity is based on emotions, compassion is grounded in character. You may see a homeless person on the corner of the street holding a sign reading, "Will Work For Food." You think to yourself, *That poor man. He's down on his luck. He doesn't have a dime to his name. He has no food to eat, no place to stay. What a shame.* Maybe your emotions are touched and you think, *I'll give him a dollar and a smile. I'll have compassion on him.*

But that's not true compassion. Compassion doesn't flow from your concern; it flows from your character. Someone has said, "Men of genius are admired. Men of wealth are envied. Men of power are feared. Men of character are trusted." We make appropriate responses to people in need because we are men and women of character, not because we are men and women of means. Character makes all the difference in the world.

It is also the trustworthy character of God that brings His compassion to us. Psalm 145:8-9 declares, "The LORD is gracious and full of compassion, slow to anger and great in mercy. The LORD is good to all, and His tender mercies are over all His works."

B. F. Westcott, the great biblical scholar, said, "Great occasions do not make heroes or cowards. They simply unveil them to the eyes of men. Silently and imperceptibly, as we wake or sleep, we grow strong or we grow weak. At last, some crisis shows us what we have become." A crisis does more than stir up our emotions; it reveals our character.

We see such a crisis in Luke 10. Jesus' story of the Good Samaritan reveals true compassion, and true character.

According to this parable, "A certain man went down from Jerusalem to Jericho, and fell among thieves, who stripped him of his clothing, wounded him, and departed, leaving him half dead. Now by chance a certain priest came down that road. And when he saw him, he passed by on the other side. Likewise a Levite, when he arrived at the place, came and looked, and passed by on the other side. But a certain Samaritan, as he journeyed, came where he was. And when he saw him, he had compassion on him" (Luke 10:30-33).

Jews hated Samaritans. They were the product of intermarriage between the Jews left after the Northern Kingdom was conquered in 721 B.C. and the Gentiles brought in to repopulate the land. No self-respecting Jew would associate with these half-breeds, and the animosity was usually returned with equal intensity on the part of the Samaritans. But the Samaritan Jesus depicted in His parable was a man of character. He refused to allow his cultural biases to stop him from doing what was right. His compassion was the consequence of *what* he was, not *who* he was.

Compassion gives rise to action

The word for "compassion" in Luke 10:33 is one of those long, unpronounceable Greek words, *splagchnizomai*. Not only is it used of the compassionate Samaritan, but it's also used in another parable, the story of the father and his prodigal son.

In Luke 15:11-24, Jesus tells the story of a son who squandered his inheritance through undisciplined living in a far country. When he came to his senses, the boy returned home to seek his father's forgiveness. Luke makes a point to relate that this father greeted his son with *splagchnizomai*, or compassion.

In both of these parables, it is significant that compassion led to action. For the Samaritan, his compassion led to binding up the wounds of the badly beaten Jew, putting him on his own donkey and then standing good for any expenses the innkeeper might incur as the man recovered. With the father, it meant bringing out the finest clothing for his son and throwing a joyful party to celebrate his return.

Compassion is not a matter of empty platitudes; it is the basis for fruitful deeds. James says, "If a brother or sister is naked and destitute of daily food, and one of you says to them, 'Depart in peace, be warmed and filled,' but you do not give them the things which are needed for the body, what does it profit?" (James 2:15-16). If we see someone who needs our help, perhaps a neighbor or someone at church, and we pity them, but we do not help them, we cannot claim to have compassion.

Compassion characterizes our Lord

When the New Testament writers wanted to reveal Jesus' compassion, they used that word *splagchnizomai*. Matthew did it again and again. He said of Jesus, "When He saw the multitudes, He was moved with compassion for them, because they were weary and scattered, like sheep having no shepherd" (Matt. 9:36). The helpless, hapless, harassed people of ancient Judaism had no one to lead them spiritually, so Jesus had compassion on them. And what follows this verse? It's the great "white harvest" challenge. "The harvest truly is plentiful, but the laborers are few" (v. 37). Jesus was not content to feel pity for these people. He was compelled to challenge His disciples to enter the harvest field and bring these sheaths of precious grain to His barns.

Matthew 14:14 also helps us understand Jesus' compassion. This passage is talking about a crowd of 5,000. "And when Jesus went out He saw a great multitude; and He was moved with compassion for them, and healed their sick." As Jesus looked at that group of 5,000 men, plus women and children, His heart stirred within Him and He healed the sick and fed the hungry. Why did He do it? Not out of pity. He did it because of compassion. He did it out of a committed love that expressed itself through actions. That's compassion—love in action.

Matthew 15:32 reveals the same in the feeding of the 4,000. Matthew tells us, "Then Jesus called His disciples to Him and said, 'I have compassion on the multitude, because they have now continued with Me three days and have nothing to eat. And I do not want to send them away hungry, lest they faint on the way.'" That's not pity; that's deep-seated compassion. Jesus did all of this out of love.

Finally there's the story in Matthew 20:29-34. As Jesus entered the city of Jericho, He encountered two blind men sitting by the side of the road. They cried out, "Have mercy on us, O Lord, Son of David!" (v. 30). The crowd told them to be quiet, but that only caused them to cry louder, "Have mercy on us, O Lord, Son of David!" (v. 31). "So Jesus stood still and called them, and said, 'What do you want Me to do for you?' They said to Him, 'Lord, that our eyes may be opened.' So Jesus had compassion and touched their eyes. And immediately their eyes received sight, and they followed Him" (vv. 32-34).

This was not simply an emotional response to someone in need; it was an expression of compassion. It came from Jesus' character, not merely from His concern. It was more related to Jesus' commitment to people rather than His feeling of pity.

Jesus' compassion and you

What Jesus felt for the hungry 5,000 of Galilee, He feels for you. The character that brought Jesus to heal two helpless blind men along the Jericho road hasn't changed. Jesus is the same yesterday, today and forever (Heb. 13:8). He has that same compassion for your need today.

When Frank Graeff was feeling all alone, desperate and despondent, he needed a lot more than pity, and so do you. He needed the compassionate Christ, and so do you. Pity may help you feel better for a few minutes, but compassion will meet your need for a lifetime, and beyond.

The compassion Jesus has for you doesn't arise from your loneliness. It doesn't stem from your feeling of abandonment. Jesus' compassion is the fruit of His character. Because of who He is, you can trust what He feels for you. He will never fake His feelings; they will be genuine because He is genuine. Isn't it time you knew there is Someone who genuinely cares for you? Jesus cares.

But Jesus' compassion for you was not just a broken heart; it was a broken body as well. We don't know His compassion from words only; we know it from His deeds. Pity did not send Jesus to Calvary; compassion did. We often think of the cross as a demonstration of the Father's love for us. "For God so loved the world that He gave His only begotten Son, that whoever believes in Him should not perish but have everlasting life" (John 3:16). That's proof of the Father's love.

But Jesus also proved His love for you. "Greater love has no one than this, than to lay down one's life for his friends" (John 15:13). Jesus died for love, not for pity. It was His compassion that took Him to Calvary. It was His love that provided for your salvation. And it is His love that meets you at the point of your loneliness.

Jesus is also the model for us to have compassion for others. He said, "A new commandment I give to you, that you love one another; as I have loved you, that you also love one another" (John 13:34). The kind of love He describes here is *agape* love, the kind of love that demands a godly character, the kind of love that is much more than pity. It is compassion.

Won't you let Jesus love you? Won't you let Him show you how much He cares? When you are all alone, when you think no one knows, no one understands, no one cares, remember that Jesus cares, He understands, He knows what you are feeling. You've not been abandoned. You're never alone as long as you have a compassionate friend. As Johnson Oatman Jr. wrote:

There's not a friend like the lowly Jesus. No, not one! No, not one!

None else could heal all our soul's diseases. No, not one! No, not one!

There's not an hour that He is not near us. No, not one! No, not one!

No night so dark but His love can cheer us. No, not one! No, not one!

CHAPTER TWO

Does Jesus Care When I'm Burdened?

Does Jesus care when my heart is pained too deeply for mirth and song;
As the burdens press, and the cares distress, and the way grows weary and long?

Some years ago I was traveling in the south of England and visited the great Canterbury Cathedral. At that point they were trying to raise funds for some much-needed repairs on the historic building. I made a small donation and in turn received a huge poster showing folks standing in front of the cathedral. It said, "We care." The message was simple. People who really care don't just talk about a problem. They do something about it. One of the ways you know someone genuinely cares for you is by what they do for you when you need them the most.

Care has become a large part of our vocabulary. We talk about health care. We talk about extended care. We talk about care givers and care receivers. Many relationships have ended with words like "You just don't care" or "He really didn't care for me." It's obvious that caring is important to us.

Yet there seems to be a tremendous shortage of caring people in the world these days.

Teen suicide has never been higher. It's not uncommon when a despondent teen takes his or her life that a note will be left behind that says something like, "It just wasn't worth it. Nobody cares if I live or die. I'm better off dead." But when we bear the burden of meaninglessness, or the burden of misunderstanding, we need to know there is someone who cares. Jesus cares when you are burdened.

When the burdens press

What weighs heavily on your mind right now? What distresses you and makes your future look hopeless? What are your burdens? Are the creditors on the phone, badgering you about where your next payment is? Are the kids sick? In fact, does it seem like they've been sick a lot lately? Does anybody care about your burdens? When you've been downsized and can't find a decent job, does anyone care?

When your marriage is under tremendous stress and you don't know how things are going to turn out, who cares? You are burdened with everything going wrong for you; do you ever wonder if anyone cares? Sure, you do. Anyone would. That's what prompted the hymn writer to ask, "Does Jesus care when my burdens press and cares distress?" You know the answer.

Luke 10:38-42 is the wonderful story of Martha and Mary. Luke tells us, "Now it happened as they went that He entered a certain village; and a certain woman named Martha welcomed Him into her house. And she had a sister called Mary, who also sat at Jesus' feet and heard His word. But Martha was distracted with much serving, and she approached Him and said, 'Lord, do You not care that my sister has left me alone to serve? Therefore, tell her to help me.' And Jesus answered and said unto her, 'Martha, Martha, you are worried and troubled about many things. But one thing is needed, and Mary has chosen that good part, which will not be taken away from her.'"

Many people have come to a different conclusion than the one I think is appropriate for this story. I feel a certain amount of empathy for Martha throughout this experience. Mary comes off pretty good, but Martha often is seen as the villain. Martha had a problem with paralyzing busyness, to be sure, and Jesus gave her some advice. But Martha is the one who teaches us how much Jesus cares for us.

"As the burdens press and the cares distress, does Jesus care?" That's the question that Martha asked Jesus. "Do You not care, Jesus, that my sister isn't helping me at all?" This story poignantly shows us what it means that Jesus cares when our burdens press and the cares distress.

The cares of leadership

Verse 38 informs us, "It happened as they went that He entered a certain village." Luke doesn't say what village it is, but we know from John 11 and 12 that it was Bethany, less than two miles from Jerusalem around the eastern and southern slopes of the Mount of Olives.

As Jesus entered the village, a "certain woman named Martha" met Him. Martha was the sister of Lazarus, the one who became a great friend to Jesus and whom He raised from the dead (John 11:43-44). She was also the sister of Mary. Of the two sisters, Martha is mentioned first, not only in Luke 10:38 but also in John 11:19-20 and in John 12:2-3. Why is this the case? Likely she was the older of the two sisters.

You also may be the older sister or the older brother in your family. Often there is more responsibility for the older child, as you've probably experienced. There is also frequently more maturity. After all, you are older. Sometimes there is more of a sense of duty as well. We can see all of those things here in the story of Martha and Mary.

Notice that it was Martha who was the hostess, not Mary. It was Martha who welcomed Jesus into their home, not Mary or even Lazarus. It was Martha who took the leadership role. What does that tell you about Martha?

Maybe it tells you that Martha was used to being in charge. She was used to taking control. She was more aggressive than Mary. She was likely more outgoing than Mary. And she was probably more responsible than her younger sister. That may be true in your family as well. The cares of leadership often come to the older sibling in ways the younger ones know nothing about. Martha was burdened down because she was responsible.

Facing responsibilities alone

Mary certainly had a tender heart. Luke 10:39 says, "And she had a sister called Mary, who also sat at Jesus' feet and heard His word." The word translated "sat" literally means to be "alongside of." This implies Mary wasn't simply listening to His teachings from a distance; rather, she had plopped herself right down next to Jesus' feet. One could hardly fault the impressionable Mary for that, but in doing so she abandoned Martha, who was left alone to do all the work. Mary wasn't lifting a finger to help.

Get the picture. Martha was older. She heard Jesus coming and took the initiative. She welcomed Him into the house. She was the one who had to see that all the needs were met. Don't miss this. Martha was about to feed her beloved Master (a rather intimidating proposition). But Jesus was not alone. Twelve disciples were with Him, and Lazarus was there, and Mary and maybe others. Dinner for more than a dozen. Get crackin', Martha. These men are hungry. Whip up a little something for this starving bunch, and do it now, and do it alone.

Martha was under stress. No microwave, no frozen vegetables, no "brown and serve" rolls. No help. Furthermore, she had to set the table and make sure the room was ready. There was a lot of work to do. Obviously Martha took her responsibilities very seriously. She was the hostess, the lone hostess. All the while, her younger sister—perhaps a sister she suspected of being a tad lazy anyway—did not greet Jesus, did not prepare the table, did not help cook the food, did not help with the serving. Instead, from Martha's perspective, Mary just lounged at Jesus' feet. She enjoyed His teaching and His company. Maybe Martha would have liked to have done that, too, but who was going to get lunch?

Wouldn't it burden you a bit if you were Martha? Wouldn't that get you just a little steamed at your sister? Mary was sitting at Jesus' feet, while Martha was doing all the work.

Luke 10:40 tells us, "But Martha was distracted with much serving, and she approached Him and said, 'Lord, do You not care that my sister has left me alone to serve? Therefore, tell her to help me.'" Martha was doing everything. That lazy sister of hers wasn't doing a thing. That word *distracted* or *encumbered* means "to draw around," "to be driven about mentally." Martha was both physically and mentally burdened.

In fact, Martha was finally burdened enough that she mustered the courage to complain to Jesus. She was doing all the work by herself. And there was Mary, just sitting at His feet. Finally, Martha exploded in frustration and anger, "Don't You care, Jesus? I am left alone to serve."

So what about you? Are you saying to yourself, "Been there, done that"?

You may have found yourself in exactly that same circumstance. It's not uncommon to be in a situation, perhaps in your family or maybe in your church, where you have to take the leadership role, and it doesn't look like anybody is going to help you. Perhaps you're entertaining someone. There's no help. You have a project due at work. There's no help. You have aging parents to care for and you have a brother and a sister, but they don't seem to be much help. Does

Jesus care? Does He care when you're burdened and working all alone?

You're serving tables. You're ministering to people's needs and they're draining you dry. The dishes are piled high. The carpet needs to be vacuumed. The dog needs to go for a walk. The kids are in front of the TV. Your husband is out doing who knows what. Does Jesus care that you're working your fingers to the bone and everybody else is just enjoying themselves? If you've asked that question, read on.

The Jesus who cares

Notice Jesus' response to Martha: "Martha, Martha, you are worried and troubled about many things" (v. 41). You are worried, Martha. You are care-full. You're full of care. The Greek word used here is *merimna.* It's used only six times in the Bible, and I always find it helpful to look at other places where a word is used to know what it means. What does it mean that Martha was "full of care"? Look at some of these other passages where this same word is used.

Consider Matthew 13:1-9. As Jesus was in a boat on the Sea of Galilee, He told the parable of the sower. The sower sowed the seed. Some fell by the wayside and the birds ate it. Some fell on stony ground and it grew up, but the sun scorched it. Some fell among the thorns, and that seed was choked out. Other seed fell on good ground and yielded its grain, some stocks a hundredfold, some sixty, some thirty.

When Jesus interpreted this parable, He said, "Now he who received seed among the thorns is he who hears the word, and the cares of this world and the deceitfulness of riches choke the word, and it becomes unfruitful" (v. 22) The words for "cares of this world" are the same words that Jesus used here when He said, "Martha, you're worried. You're full of care." By the way, isn't it interesting the two examples Jesus chose for those things that choke the effectiveness of the Word of God in our lives—the cares of this world and the deceitfulness of riches? That's very telling.

Paul often spoke about all he had to endure for the sake of the Gospel. In 2 Corinthians 11 he mentioned being sleepless, hungry, thirsty, naked, in perils in the wilderness and perils in the sea, among false brethren and many more difficult situations. Then he says, "Beside those things that are without, that which cometh upon me daily, the care of all the churches (v. 28, KJV). Notice that it's not the "care" of the churches but the "cares"; the word there is *merimna*. He's talking about the troubles, the burdens of all the churches. It's the same word used in Martha's story.

Martha was burdened in her mind. She was troubled about many cares. Maybe it wasn't the first time Mary had left Martha to do all the work. She was wondering why Jesus didn't do something about it. Have you ever wondered that yourself? Why doesn't Jesus do something about your burdens? Why doesn't He get you some help, or at least a little appreciation? Jesus has a marvelously sympathetic heart, but sometimes it seems like He just doesn't care.

There's a wonderful story about Tom Landry when he was the head coach of the Dallas Cowboys. The story concerned the late Ohio State football coach Woody Hayes, who was fired for striking an opposing player on the sidelines—during a nationally televised bowl game, no less. It was a dumb thing to do, but it was too late. The press had a field day. They tarred and feathered the former Buckeyes coach. Few people in America could have felt lower than Woody Hayes did at the time. He not only lost control during the game, but he also lost his job, he lost his dignity, and he lost respect.

At the end of that season, a large banquet was held for professional athletes. Of course, Tom Landry, as a winning coach, was invited. Everybody could bring one guest. Do you know whom Tom Landry brought to that banquet? Woody Hayes, the man everyone was encouraged to hate and criticize.

I see that same attitude in the Lord Jesus. This story indicates how Jesus cared for Martha at this low point. She was overburdened and stressed out, but Jesus cared.

We're prone to criticize Martha because she did not choose the better part. We look at her and say, "Martha, what are you complaining about?" But what Martha needed was care, not criticism.

If you've been there, you know exactly how Martha must have felt. You've recognized what it's like to be doing the work when there are plenty of others around to do it, but they aren't helping. That's why it's important to take note of Jesus' response in light of how very much Martha needed someone to care for her. Jesus said, "One thing is needed, and Mary has chosen that good part, which will not be taken away from her" (Luke 10:42). Jesus did not criticize Martha for her complaint. He understood it. He empathized with it. His whole life resonated with it. It was a genuine complaint and Jesus did not minimize it. He simply cared so deeply for Martha that He desired what was better for her.

One thing needed

What did Jesus mean when He said, "One thing is needed"? What He did not mean is clear. Not one more thing to serve is needed. Not one more course, not one more vegetable at this elaborate meal, not one more set of dishes, not one more relish tray, one more meat plate, one more tray of dessert. Jesus was not saying one more thing was necessary to complete this meal, nor one more setting at the table.

The one needed thing was heartfelt devotion to the Lord. The one necessary thing was not the political correctness of the table setting, the seasoning of the meat, the right selections of Middle Eastern pastries. The one thing that was needed was time with the Master—time to adore the person of Jesus Christ, time to absorb His presence.

Can there be anything better than true devotion to the Lord, true adoration of the Savior? Mary had chosen that part. Did Jesus care that nobody was helping Martha? Yes, He cared enough to say, "Martha, Martha." He wasn't being accusatory. Jesus said it with tender affection, with real compassion. He understood Martha's need to act responsibly, but He didn't want her to miss out on the best things by being burdened with the good things. He was the best thing that would happen in Martha's life that day. It wasn't that serving was unimportant; it was very important. It just wasn't the most important, and Jesus cares enough for us to want what's best for us.

In the early 1700s, Philip Doddridge wrote, "How gentle are God's commands! How kind His precepts are! Come, cast your burdens on the Lord and trust His constant care. Why should this anxious load press down your weary mind? Haste to your Heavenly Father's throne and sweet refreshment find. His goodness stands approved, unchanged from day to day. I'll drop my burdens at His feet and bear a song away."

The Burden Bearer

So what burdens you today? What is it that is weighing you down a bit? Are you burdened about your children? Proverbs 22:6 has an answer for that. Jesus cares about your kids. Are you burdened about your finances? Psalm 112:1-4 talks about that. Jesus cares when you're a little short on cash. Are you burdened about your health? Psalm 42:11 says, "Why are you cast down, O my soul? And why are you disquieted within me? Hope in God."

If you're burdened with anything today, listen to this advice: "casting all your care upon Him, for He cares for you" (1 Pet. 5:7). Jesus cares when you are burdened,

He really does. He cares when no one else seems to be shouldering the responsibility and you are all alone. Jesus cares. But He cares enough for you that He bids you to get rid of whatever burdens you, and the best way to get rid of your burden is to hand it to Him.

The old hymn is as right as ever: "I must tell Jesus all of my trials; I cannot bear these burdens alone. In my distress He kindly will help me; He ever loves and cares for His own."

Have you experienced His care for you? Have you rolled your burdens onto Him? When the workload is high and the help is scarce, do you fret and fuss, or do you trust the One who cares for you? Jesus told Martha not to worry but simply to trust Him. That didn't necessarily mean that Mary would from then on share in the workload. It doesn't appear that she did. In fact, on a subsequent visit to Martha's house after Jesus raised Lazarus from the dead, John 12:1 says, "There they made Him supper, and Martha served." There was no mention of Mary helping. But there was no complaint from Martha either.

Martha was still in the business of serving, but now she was serving with a whole new attitude. Lazarus was engaged in conversation with the other men. Lazarus was around the table eating. Mary took a pound of very costly ointment of spikenard and anointed Jesus' feet. Mary was at the table anointing. But Martha—well, Martha was still at the table serving. And even though her workload had not changed, her attitude had. There was not one word of complaint.

She took her responsibility seriously, but now she was convinced that Jesus truly cared for her and she never questioned His care again.

Does Jesus care for you? Yes, He does. He surely does. Spend some quality time with Jesus today, as Mary did. Fall in love with Him all over again. Enjoy His presence. But take comfort in the fact that when you are burdened or when you are frustrated or when you are anxious, you are loved. You are the object of God's tender care. Don't doubt it and don't forget it. Jesus cares for you.

CHAPTER THREE

Does Jesus Care When I Worry?

Does Jesus care when my way is dark with a nameless dread and fear?

As the daylight fades into deep night shades, does He care enough to be near?

Do you ever worry? We all do. Remember Alfred E. Newman? He's the cartoon character who used to say, "Me, worry?"

Technically, worry is a sin. But it's one of those seemingly "acceptable" sins. You know the kind—we all know it's sin, but we all accept a little bit of it. Worry is one of those human tendencies that many of us won't be rid of until we're in heaven. Worry seems to be everywhere. It's a universal problem.

And what are the things we worry about? Everything. You name it. We worry about our children. We worry about how to make ends meet. We worry about losing our job. We worry about offending our in-laws. We worry about retirement. We worry about the friends our kids hang out with. We worry about the national debt. We worry about that big decision coming up in our life. We worry about global warming. We worry about caring for our elderly parents.

If you can think about it, you can worry about it.

I don't think the consequences of worry are as intense as the consequences for sins like murder or incest. But sin is sin and sin always has consequences. For those who worry, perhaps the biggest consequence is living in constant fear.

Fear and worry can be deadly. In his book *The Solid Rock Construction Company*, Adam Robinson tells this helpful story. He writes, "Death was walking into a city one morning when a man stopped him and asked him what he was doing. 'I'm going into the city to claim 10,000 people,' Death answered. 'That's horrible,' said the man. 'It's horrible that you would take 10,000 people.' 'Look,' Death said, 'get off my back. Taking people when their time has come is my job. Today I have to get my 10,000.'

"Later that day as Death was coming out of the city, the man met him again. He was furious. 'You told me this morning that you were going to take 10,000 people, but 70,000 died today.' Death said, 'Don't get on my case. I only took my 10,000. Worry and anxiety killed all the rest.'"

Sometimes the things we fear most—the things we worry about most—we can't even name. They're just a shapeless, intangible dread. It's like a constant gloom that hangs over your head. You just know something bad is going to happen to you, but you don't know what it is. You're not a psychic, but you are scared.

The comfort of prayer

Does Jesus care? When you worry and fear and you can't even put your finger on what's bothering you, does Jesus care? Well, there's a psalm that addresses that question. It's Psalm 102. This psalm begins, "Hear my prayer, O LORD, and let my cry come to You." I think you'll find answers to the problem of worry in this psalm. Let's take a look.

The writer of Psalm 102 begins by begging God to listen to his concerns. His plea, "Hear my prayer," is genuine and tender. When you're in real need, you want to do more than fret; you want to pray. But you want to be confident that God hears you when you pray. That's important.

It was very common for psalmists to cry out to God and ask Him to hear them. David says in Psalm 27:7, "Hear, O LORD, when I cry with my voice! Have mercy also upon me and answer me." Hear. Have mercy. Answer. In Psalm 39:12 he declares, "Hear my prayer, O LORD, and give ear to my cry; do not be silent at my tears." Notice his plea again: Hear. Give ear. Answer. And what about Psalm 55:1-2? "Give ear to my prayer, O God, and do not hide Yourself from my supplication. Attend to me, and hear me." Like an echo, we hear the same plea again: Give ear. Attend. Hear me.

It's obvious that those who wrote the psalms were often in distress, worried and perhaps even fearful. They were concerned about things that might not have been tangible, but were real nonetheless. In the midst of all their fear and worry, however, the first thing David and the others did was to go to God in prayer. They cried out, "Hear me." When you're all alone and you're worried and fearful, do what the psalmists did: pray and be confident that God cares enough to hear. As long as God is on the throne, comfort is on the way.

He cares for the elderly

Perhaps you're easing down the far side of life's hill. The years have come and magically gone and you don't know how many days you have left. You're a bit worried about it. Does Jesus still care for you? He surely does. Let God's Word help you overcome that worry.

Apparently the psalmist in Psalm 102 was frail. Consider what he says in verse 3: "My days are consumed like smoke, and my bones are burned like a hearth." He was depressed. He was tired of living. He viewed his days as being consumed—not lived, just consumed. They were wasting away as a moth eats a leaf. So substantial was the psalmist's grief that he describes his remaining days as being tenuous as smoke. He is so old and so lifeless that he has become like the embers on a hearth, almost burned out.

Maybe this describes your situation. You've reached those golden years of your 80s or even 90s. It seems to you as if your life has blown away like smoke, while your body has remained as a smoldering ember. You can't do the things you once did. In fact, everything about your body hurts, and if it doesn't hurt, it doesn't work. You can't drive anymore, run anymore, work in the garden anymore. You can't even get out to go to the store to do your own grocery shopping. You're totally dependent upon someone else. Does Jesus care?

Well, if you're worried about these things because they describe you, I have good news. You're not the first to worry about advancing age, and you won't be the last. The psalmist knew what to do, and so can you. You have to take your worries and fears to the Lord in prayer. Ask Him to make Himself real to you today, as if He were in the room with you. Talk with Him. Read His Word, and if you can't do that anymore, have someone from church come and read the Bible to you. Old age need not be an impediment to fellowshipping with the Lord. In fact, it can be a great benefit to you. You may find your intimacy with the Lord grow as you are less mobile and have less opportunity to interact with other people.

Jesus does care for you, even when it becomes harder to get up every morning and your old bones are weak and brittle like burned-out embers on a hearth. When you need Him the most, you can experience His care the most. "As the daylight fades into deep night shades, does He care enough to be near?" You need to know that Jesus cares for you and He is nearer to you now than ever before.

He cares for the ill

Psalm 102:4 describes a person in the final days of illness or old age. "My heart is stricken and withered like grass, so that I forget to eat my bread." The old psalmist's heart was weak. The healthy heart of his youth was now a tired, worn-out muscle. It was like grass that is curled up and ready to die. His energy was almost gone. His beauty had faded. His freshness, his joy—all those things—were behind him. His best days were the days he had already lived. His heart was beginning to fail him. He was shriveled up and tired. His skin was full of wrinkles and his body was frail and weak. His mind often played tricks on him and his appetite was almost destroyed. His will to eat and to live was virtually gone.

Do you know anybody like this aging psalmist? Does this describe someone you know and love? Maybe it describes you. Perhaps you have to depend on "Meals on Wheels" to get a hot lunch anymore. Or even worse, you've lost your ability to eat and you must depend on IVs for feeding you your sustenance. When your mind is clear you always wonder, "Does anybody really care about me? Do my children still love me? Is anybody interested in me?" Maybe you're even beginning to wonder whether Jesus really cares for you.

Well, if you've allowed those thoughts to run through your mind, remember that so did the psalmist. At the end of his life he also pondered, "Does anybody care for me?" He simply groaned and wondered. Have you done that?

Verse 5 tells it all. "Because of the sound of my groaning my bones cling to my skin." How tragic, but how very poetic. The sounds of silence in his life have now given way to the sounds of groaning. This psalmist once suffered in silence, but now he can suffer in silence no longer. His pain was so great and his suffering so intense that he simply agonizes. He cries out and wonders if anybody is listening to him. Does anybody care that he is in such pain?

The poor man says, "My bones cling to my skin." He was nothing but skin and bones. That layer of fat that once covered his skin and warmed him during winter nights was now pretty well gone. His appearance was best described as smoke-dried, withered and burned up. The pall of death was hanging heavily over his life.

You may know exactly what this is like. Perhaps you're fighting the most difficult battle of your life. In fact, maybe you're fighting the battle for life itself. You want to know if you have to fight that battle alone. You want to know if Jesus really cares. Does He still walk with you in your life? He did in your youth. Has He abandoned you now in your illness? Does Jesus really care?

That's a sincere and important question. When it seems as if no one else cares that you're ill, you need to know the answer is "Yes, He cares!" Jesus is there for you. He is there to hold your hand in the darkest hours of your night. He is there for you in your final days, just as He was in the days of your youth. Jesus is there because Jesus cares. You will never outgrow your need for His care or outlive His need to care for you. Jesus cares for you even when you're ill.

He cares for the lonely

Maybe you're not sick. Maybe you're just alone. You live by yourself. You're in a house or an apartment and you're there all by yourself. Nobody else is near. You don't even know the neighbors across the street or across the hall. It's dark outside. It's dreary in the hallway. You have two, three, even four locks on your door. Nobody ever seems to come by. Nobody checks on you. Nobody gives you a call to find out how you're doing. If the phone rings, you're afraid to answer it. You have some friends, but you don't see them very often. Maybe you see them at church once a week, but it seems like they never visit you.

You're feeling a little down and you wonder if anybody really cares. When the night falls and you have no one to share your evening with, you wonder whether it's all worthwhile. Is life really worth living? Your life is so lonely, you wonder if anybody would miss you if you weren't around. Does Jesus care for you then?

The psalmist felt that way too. In Psalm 102:6-7 he writes, "I am like a pelican of the wilderness; I am like an owl of the desert. I lie awake, and am like a sparrow alone on the housetop."

A pelican. The word translated "pelican" is really the Hebrew word meaning "to vomit." It refers to the pelican's practice of regurgitating its own food into the deep bill of its young. That enables the pelican to remain in desolate places for long periods of time. It's a mournful bird. The image here is one of desolation and solitude.

That's why the psalmist says, "I'm just like that bird. Nobody ever comes to visit me anymore. I'm here all by myself. I'm like an owl in the desert, living in the ruins, hooting discordantly at no one, spending a lifetime in melancholy and loneliness." He uses the most commonly understood emblems of gloom and wretchedness—the things people in his day would understand.

He says, "I lie awake." He tried to sleep, but sleep wouldn't come. Have you ever tried to sleep and couldn't find sleep? You're so worried about what's going to happen to you. The pain is so great. The loneliness is so severe. Nobody ever comes around. Does anybody care?

The psalmist muses, "I'm alone like the sparrow on the housetop. I'm distant. I'm away from everybody. I'm unapproachable. I'm here by myself. Nobody else is here and nobody else is coming."

You may be reading this right now and you're saying, "My goodness! It's as if I could have written those words. Those words were written about me. Here I am, languishing in my sickbed. I'm spending my final days in the hospital. I'm at a hospice. I'm living alone, all alone. It's like the psalmist had been reading my mail."

Day after day you're stuck at home. Your meager meals aren't very nutritious and so you're nothing but skin and bones. Your days are coming to an end just as rapidly as smoke dissipates from a fire. You can't eat. Your appetite is gone. You can't even suffer in silence anymore. You cry out, but no one answers. No one comes to visit you. No one cares.

If you've felt like that, read these words from Psalm 42: "Why are you cast down, O my soul? And why are you disquieted within me? Hope in God, for I shall yet praise Him for the help of His countenance. O my God, my soul is cast down within me; therefore, I will remember You . . . . The

Lord will command His lovingkindness in the daytime, and in the night His song shall be with me—a prayer to the God of my life" (vv. 5-6, 8).

These words are a cry to God from the psalmist who was all alone, just like you. He was greatly depressed, just like you. But he had hope. And maybe you're asking, "What was his hope?" His only hope, my Friend, was exactly what your only hope is. It's my only hope too.

And what is that hope? What cheered the psalmist and gave him comfort? What was the only hope he had when he was all alone at night? It was this. God was there for him. God cared about him. God loved him. In fact, God cared for and loved him so much, all he had to do was pray and he could talk directly with His dearest Friend. The only hope he had was to cling to the God who was clinging to him.

A light in the dark

The God who cared for the psalmist in Psalm 42 cared for the psalmist in Psalm 102. God cares for you the very same way. When your way is dark, commit your way to Him. Trust in Him. Delight yourself in Him. Read your Bible. Be open and honest with God in prayer. Speak right out to Him. Talk with Him as you would your best friend. God will bring forth every righteous light to your path. That's His promise of Psalm 37.

When you're all alone and you think nobody cares, when your life is filled with a dread and you can't even put your finger on what's causing it, just remember this: Jesus cares and He can take away your fears.

As William C. Poole said in his old hymn, "Just when I need Him, Jesus is near; just when I falter, just when I fear; ready to help me, ready to cheer, just when I need Him most."

When you're all alone, when your way is dark, when the daylight fades in the deep night shades, what should you do? Do what God's Word suggests. Cling tightly to this eternal truth: Jesus cares for you.

William R. Marshall, in his delightful little book *Eternity Shut in a Span*, tells the story of a woman who had been having trouble getting to sleep at night because she feared burglars. "One night her husband heard a noise in the house, so he went downstairs to investigate. Sure enough, when he got there he found a burglar. 'Good evening,' said the man of the house to the burglar. 'I'm pleased to see you. Come upstairs and meet my wife. She's been expecting you for the last ten years.'"

It's true, isn't it? We often worry about things that are never going to happen. I understand why I do it, and it's probably the same with you. We do it because we're concerned. We do it because we're all alone. We do it because we think nobody cares. But you don't need to worry about the things you can't control. Let Jesus control them for you and there's no cause to worry. Jesus cares for you. He really does. He loves you more than you can understand. He cares more deeply for you than anyone else does. If you're worried that nobody cares, take heart. Jesus cares!

CHAPTER FOUR

Does Jesus Care When I've Failed?

Does Jesus care when I've tried and failed to resist some temptation strong;

When for my deep grief I find no relief, though my tears flow all the night long?

A man went off to the Black Hawk War as a captain and, through no fault of his own, returned as a private. That brought an end to his military career. Then his little shop in a country village "winked out," as he used to say, marking his failure as a businessman. As a lawyer in Springfield, Illinois, he was too impractical, too unpolished, too temperamental to be a success. Turning to politics, he was defeated in his campaign for the legislature, defeated in his first attempt to be nominated for Congress, defeated in his application to be Commissioner of the General Land Office, defeated in the senatorial election of 1854, defeated in his aspirations for the vice presidency in 1856, and defeated again in the senatorial election of 1858. Abraham Lincoln was finally elected president of the United States in 1860, but it was a route strewn with a multitude of failures.

Most of us know what it's like to fail. In fact, failure is a part of life, but that doesn't make it any easier, does it? It's painful when we fail in politics or a job, but it becomes even more difficult to accept when we fail at marriage or we fail to witness to a friend and that friend dies without knowing the Lord. Failure is hard to accept. And isn't it true that sometimes we beat up on ourselves when we fail?

If I were to ask you to make a list of your ten worst mistakes—your biggest failures in life—and then to prioritize them, I wonder which ones would come to the top. Your list would likely be different from mine. I'm not going to tell you what I'd put at the top of my list, but I know what one fellow would put at the top of his list.

It was New Year's Day, 1929. Roy Regals made football history that day because of his colossal failure. You may remember it, or at least have heard about it.

While Regals was playing football for the University of California, he grabbed a Georgia Tech fumble. That was good. Unfortunately, he was spun around by a would-be tackler and took off on a gallop going the wrong direction. That was bad. He was running to the wrong end zone. For a moment, the other players simply froze. They couldn't believe that Regals was running the wrong way. They just couldn't believe their eyes. Then one of Regals's teammates took off in pursuit, tackling the confused young man just before he would have crossed his own line and scored for the other team.

Can you top that mistake? Maybe you can. What's the real whopper in your life?

Robert Frost was one of the greatest American poets, yet he labored for 20 years without any fame or success at all. He was a failure for 20 years.

Do you know that when Enrico Caruso, the famous Italian tenor, took voice lessons as a young boy, his voice cracked so much that his instructor said he ought to give up? We're all glad that he didn't.

And do you know that a newspaper editor once fired a young cartoonist because he said he lacked imagination? That young cartoonist, by the way, was Walt Disney. Talk about people making big mistakes!

So what are your big mistakes? What are your failures in life? Maybe your failure is you married the wrong man or woman. Maybe you failed to answer God's call on your life. You've known it for 20 or 30 or more years and have been in a wrestling match with God since day one. Maybe you failed in raising your children. They've drifted away from God and you're wondering what the problem was when you were raising them. Maybe you failed in business. Yours may have been a moral failure in your life and perhaps nobody knows it but you and one other person.

What do you do when you really mess things up? What's it like to be a real failure before God? And when we are real failures before God, does anybody care? More to the point, does Jesus care?

He cares for sinners

The apostle Paul said, "I thank Christ Jesus our Lord who has enabled me, because

He found me faithful, putting me into the ministry, although I was formerly a blasphemer, a persecutor, and an insolent man; but I obtained mercy because I did it ignorantly in unbelief. And the grace of our Lord was exceedingly abundant, with faith and love which are in Christ Jesus" (1 Tim. 1:12-13).

Jesus cares enough about us to love us even when we sin, and He forgives us even after we sin. First John 1:9 says, "If we confess our sins, He is faithful and just to forgive us our sins and to cleanse us from all unrighteousness."

So does Jesus care for you when you're a failure? Yes, He does. Psalm 86:5 declares, "For You, LORD, are good and ready to forgive; and abundant in mercy to all those who call upon You." All you have to do to be forgiven by God is to repent of your sin, to confess it as sin, to call on God and ask for forgiveness.

Nehemiah 9:17 describes God this way: "You are God, ready to pardon, gracious and merciful, slow to anger, abundant in kindness." God loves you, my Friend. And Jesus cares for you, even though you have been a failure. In fact, the bigger the failure you have been, the deeper His love. God's love is sufficient for all your needs, but the deeper you have fallen into the pit, the deeper God's love has to go to pull you out.

He cares for the moral failures

But what if your sin is a moral failure? Often we view moral failures as the worst kind. Does Jesus really care when you are a moral failure? Yes, He does. Jesus cares.

Remember the story of the rich young ruler? He came to Jesus with a seemingly impeccable moral background. He said, "Good Teacher, what shall I do that I may inherit eternal life?" (Mark 10:17). Jesus responded, "You know the commandments: 'Do not commit adultery,' 'Do not murder,' 'Do not steal,' 'Do not bear false witness,' 'Do not defraud,' 'Honor your father and your mother'" (v. 19).

This wealthy, moral man then said to Jesus, "Teacher, all these have I observed from my youth" (v. 20). Still, this man was a moral failure. He couldn't resist the temptation to be proud of his goodness, his morality. Because of this, he was a failure. He couldn't admit his need, and thus he was the only man who came to Jesus with a serious problem who walked away unhappy.

Did Jesus continue to care about this moral misfit? He certainly did. Jesus cares for failures. Verse 21 tells us, "Then Jesus, looking at him, loved him."

You see, Jesus cares enough to continue to love us even when we are moral failures. When we have failed to resist "some temptation strong," Christ doesn't simply write us off as a lost cause. Instead, He loves us. He genuinely cares for us.

All right, so you've had a lapse in your life. That doesn't mean Jesus doesn't love you anymore. What He wants you to do is confess that lapse, get that sin behind you, repent of it, make it right and move on. Jesus loves you. Does Jesus really care when we're failures? Yes, He does. He cares enough to forgive us. Forgiveness is proof positive that Jesus cares. He can forgive you, if you ask Him.

Who can forgive sins?

There are many ways that we can fail. Maybe you've failed to provide for your family. You may be reading this book in your car because, well, you don't have a home. You have no place to call home, so your car is your home.

Or it may be that your problem isn't that you don't have a home. Your problem is that you do, but you're not there. You're living with someone else. You've left your wife and your children. You've disgraced your family. Any way you look at it, you're a moral failure.

Who has the power to forgive failures like you? Mark 2:1-13 records the story of the paralyzed man who was let down through the roof of a house Jesus was in by his four friends. When Jesus saw his faith, He said, "Son, your sins are forgiven you" (v. 5). The scribes and the Pharisees then asked, "Who can forgive sins but God alone?" (v. 7). So Jesus replied, "'But that you may know that the Son of Man has power on earth to forgive sins'—He said to the paralytic, 'I say to you, arise, take up your bed, and go your way to your house'" (vv. 10-11).

Ultimately only God can forgive you. He can take away that moral failure in your life. He loves you so much that He sent His Son, Jesus, to Calvary to pay the penalty for your moral failure. Does Jesus care? Absolutely. Does He care when you have sinned? Does He care when you have failed Him? Absolutely. In fact, He cares enough about you to love you still and to forgive you of your sin.

If He didn't care for you, He'd let you fail again with no possibility of ever being forgiven, but He doesn't. He loves you. He forgives you because He cares for you.

No limits allowed

The greatest failure of all time was on the part of the mob who crucified our Lord on the cross of Calvary. But while they were failing, Jesus was forgiving. Have you noticed that? He said, "Father, forgive them, for they do not know what they do" (Luke 23:34). Forgiveness follows failure when you have someone who cares.

Does Jesus really care when we're failures? Yes, He does. He cares enough to justify us. He cares enough to treat us as if we had never failed. He cares enough to make things right again.

Consider Peter. Jesus told Peter that he would try but fail to resist a temptation, and Jesus was right. John 18 reports that by the time the rooster had crowed, Peter denied the Lord three times. Now that's a failure. Peter was a great failure. He attempted to resist temptation but he couldn't do it. He failed.

"And Simon Peter followed Jesus, and so did another disciple. Now that disciple was known to the high priest, and went with Jesus into the courtyard of the high priest. But Peter stood at the door outside. Then the other disciple, who was known to the high priest, went out and spoke to her who kept the door, and brought Peter in. Then the servant girl who kept the door said to

Peter, 'You are not also one of this Man's disciples, are you?' He said, 'I am not'" (vv. 15-17). Notice how quickly Peter responded. "It's not me. I'm not the one."

John 18:25 continues, "Now Simon Peter stood and warmed himself. Therefore they said to him, 'You are not also one of His disciples, are you?' He denied it and said, 'I am not!'" When Peter denied the Lord the third time (v. 27), the cock crowed.

Peter was not a super saint, to be sure. He was just somebody like you and me. He was also, at times, a colossal failure. He said, "Lord, I'll go with You everywhere. I'll do whatever You want me to do. And I absolutely, positively will never deny You. There is no way this is ever going to happen." But it did happen.

Yet Jesus continued to love Peter, even after His disciple became a failure. Jesus picked him up. He dusted him off. He forgave him. Go to the end of John, chapter 21, and see Jesus talking to Peter there, asking Peter if he loves Him. Peter had denied the Lord three times. He had failed the Lord three times. Now, he is given the opportunity to say to the Lord Jesus, "I love you." It's no coincidence that opportunity came three times.

Peter became one of the greatest preachers in the early church. He was the principal spokesman during the early days of Christianity after the Lord's resurrection (Acts 2:14-36; 3:12-26; 4:8-12). Are you surprised? Probably not, when you consider that Jesus cares.

Could there be exceptions? Are there people whom Jesus doesn't care about, people He will refuse to forgive?

First Corinthians 6:9-10 declares, "Do you not know that that the unrighteous will not inherit the kingdom of God? Do not be deceived. Neither fornicators, nor idolaters, nor adulterers, nor homosexuals, nor sodomites, nor thieves, nor covetous, nor drunkards, nor revilers, nor extortioners will inherit the kingdom of God."

That's pretty tough, isn't it? These failures are some of the worst kind. And yet verse 11 goes on to say, "And such were some of you. But you were washed, but you were sanctified, but you were justified in the name of the Lord Jesus Christ and by the Spirit of our God."

Does Jesus care for those who fail? Just ask these people who used to be slanderers, used to be homosexuals, used to be idolaters or adulterers, used to be male prostitutes. Ask them. They will tell you. He cares enough not to excuse their sin but, when they genuinely repent of it, He cares enough to justify them, to treat them as if they had never sinned. He cares enough to save and to treat us as if we were righteous. He cares for those who are sexually immoral. My Friend, Jesus cares. Jesus doesn't care for their sin, but He cares for the sinner. Jesus cares.

This means you

What about you? Does Jesus care when you've tried and failed to resist some temptation strong? When in your deep grief, you find no relief, though your tears flow all the night long?

When you sin against the Lord God, when you fall into some deep sin, when you stumble at some deep temptation and your pastor doesn't know, maybe your children don't even know, maybe nobody knows but you—when you fall into temptation, does Jesus care? What do you think? Jesus cares.

Let's understand temptation correctly. I think Erwin Lutzer was right. He said, "Temptation is God's magnifying glass. It shows us how much work He has left to do in us." Temptation isn't sin. Giving into temptation is sin. When we give into temptation, it only shows us how much more God has to do in our lives to make us like His Son. Jesus cares for you even when you are tempted and fall.

So what does this have to do with you? I think it has everything to do with you. You and I were not the first failures in this world, and we won't be the last. For Moses, the failure was murder. For Elijah, the failure was deep depression. For Peter, the failure was public denial. For Samson, the failure was a recurring problem with lust. For Thomas, it was the problem of cynical doubting. For Jacob, it was the problem of deception. We all have our failures.

What do these people have in common with you and me? They were losers, failures, every one of them. They were people who loved God and God loved them, and yet they failed. If you haven't failed the Lord yet, just wait. If you haven't given into temptation, just wait. If you haven't become a moral mess, just wait. The likelihood of giving in to one temptation or another is extremely high.

If you have failed the Lord, if you have given into temptation, if you are a moral mess today, you don't need to despair. I don't want to minimize your failure. It is significant. But what I want to do is maximize the Savior. He is more significant than your failure. Jesus deeply cares for you and He wants to help you. He came to give you life, my Friend. He came to give you abundant life. He came to give you a life better than anything you've seen thus far. All you have to do to have that life is to trust Him as your Savior, to confess your sin and receive His forgiveness for that sin. All you have to do is accept His offer of salvation, to allow Him to use you in a new way—a way that honors Him. In short, all you have to do is recognize that Jesus cares for you and accept His care.

So what about it? Are you a failure? In some way, you probably are. We all are, to some extent. Have you failed today, even though you may be a believer? Have you failed to live for the Lord the way you want to? Have you failed to resist temptation?

We're all failures. But you need to know that failure is not the end. Failure doesn't mean you're been defeated. Failure can be only a temporary setback. Jesus loves you. He cares for you. He came to die for you. He was successful in giving His life to pay the penalty for the sin of failures like you and me.

If you are a failure, life isn't over. If you've lost the battle with temptation and now you wonder if Jesus really cares, take heart. He does. If you need to get something right with the Lord, why don't you do so right now? Just tell Him what temptation you've given in to. Tell Him it's sin. Tell Him you know it's sin. Ask Him to forgive you. He cares enough to forgive you of all your sins and to cleanse you from their lingering effects.

If you've failed and you ask Jesus to forgive you, do you know what He'll do? He'll do what any caring person would do. He'll forgive you, if you really mean it. If you are genuine, He'll pick you up, He'll dust you off, He'll use you again, because Jesus cares. Jesus deeply cares for you, even when you fail.

CHAPTER FIVE

Does Jesus Care When I Sorrow?

Does Jesus care when I've said good-by to the dearest on earth to me,

And my sad heart aches till it nearly breaks—is it aught to Him? Does He see?

I began my ministry at Back to the Bible in August of 1990. Just two months later, Mrs. Theodore Epp went to be with her Lord. I had the honor of conducting her funeral, upholding her memory and uplifting the name of the Lord Jesus. It was a very hard time for us here at Back to the Bible. Her husband, Theodore Epp, the founder of Back to the Bible, had died just five years earlier. It's easy at those times in life to ask, "Does Jesus care?" Does it really touch Him when we're grieving, or is He just an intercessor? We know He is at the right hand of the Father, our Advocate, our Coming King. We know He is doing His job. But is He just doing it, or is He doing it with caring concern for us?

This past year, in about a six-week period of time, I received news of six of my dear friends who lost a battle with cancer or with old age. They lost the battle of life. Now they're in Glory. Most of these friends were dear, faithful prayer warriors. They were prayer partners with us here at Back to the Bible. They were loyal financial supporters of this ministry. We miss them.

Yet I always receive such news with mixed emotions. I'm happy for my friends, because now they're with the Lord. But I'm sad for their families, because their loved ones miss them so very deeply.

Maybe you've recently lost someone who is very dear to you. Perhaps it was a spouse or a young child, a father or mother. Does Jesus really care? Is He really touched with the feeling of your anguish? Does He feel your pain? Does He grieve with you?

The answer to these questions is yes on every count. Jesus cares. He is not simply putting in His time at the Father's right hand, interceding for us and praying for us. He cares for us. Remember, Jesus is truly God. As God, Jesus possesses all the full range of divine emotions. That means He is not a robot. He is not an uncaring, unfeeling deity. He is the caring, compassionate God. He is a person who loves you and who feels deeply everything you feel.

How do I know this? Is it just something I was taught years ago in Sunday school and therefore believe today? No, I know Jesus cares for two reasons. First, I have experienced His gentle care in my life. He has been a Care Giver to me. But more than that, I know Jesus cares because the Bible says so. Let's investigate.

Jesus is a feeling person

Psalm 86:15 reminds us, "You, O Lord, are a God full of compassion, and gracious, longsuffering and abundant in mercy and truth." This verse describes the character of God, not just the Father but the Trinity. Each member of the Godhead is full of compassion. Each One is gracious. Each is longsuffering and abundant in mercy and truth. You cannot segment the personality of God. What is true for the character of the Father is also true for the character of the Son and the Spirit.

The feeling character of God is reiterated in Psalm 145:8-9: "The LORD is gracious and full of compassion, slow to anger and great in mercy. The LORD is good to all and His tender mercies are over all His works."

When you read your Bible, you can't help but be struck with the fact that God really is a feeling person. He is not just up there pulling strings and wondering what's happening. As God, Jesus loves us and He is deeply involved in our lives. That's the Bible's testimony to the caring Jesus. We know He loves us because we have experienced His love, and besides, the Bible says so. Remember the little chorus you learned as a child? It's still true today. "Jesus loves me, this I know, for the Bible tells me so." God the Son loves me. He really loves me. Jesus is God, and God cares.

But Jesus possesses the full range of human emotions, just as He possesses the full range of divine emotions. He is truly God and truly man. That means that just as He is not a robot God, He is not a robot man. He is not an uncaring God; so, too, He is not an uncaring person. He is a very feeling, loving, compassionate man.

Matthew 9:35-36 records, "And Jesus went about all the cities and villages, teaching in their synagogues, preaching the gospel of the kingdom, and healing every sickness and every disease among the people. But when He saw the multitudes, He was moved with compassion for them, because they were weary and scattered, like sheep having no shepherd." Let me ask you, does that sound like a Jesus who doesn't care for you?

And don't forget Matthew 14:13-14: "He departed from there by boat to a deserted place by Himself. But when the multitudes heard it, they followed Him on foot from the cities. And when Jesus went out He saw a great multitude; and He was moved with compassion for them, and healed their sick." Does that sound to you like Jesus is unfeeling? These are not the acts of a man without compassion. Jesus cares. He really cares.

Remember also the account of the leper who came to Jesus and knelt at His feet and said, "If you are willing, You can make me clean" (Mark 1:40). "And Jesus, moved with compassion, put out His hand and touched him, and said to him, "I am willing; be cleansed" (v. 41). Does Jesus care? Just ask this restored leper when you get to heaven.

What about me?

Now maybe you're thinking, *All right, Jesus was compassionate. He was a man of great love. He healed the sick. He restored sight to the blind. But what does that have to do with me today? How has He demonstrated His compassion to me?*

That's a good question, and God's Word has a good answer. The Bible reveals that

Jesus suffered for you. He bled for you. He died for you. He had compassion for you. He did it all for you so that you could trust Him and go to heaven when you die.

Ephesians 5:2 reminds us that Christ loved us and gave Himself for us. He gave Himself as an offering and as a sacrifice to God. That's what Jesus did for you. That's how He shows His compassion for you. He offered Himself for you because He loves you.

In the last book of the Bible, John describes Jesus as the faithful witness, the firstborn from the dead, the ruler over the kings of the earth, the One who loved us and washed us from our sins in His own blood (Rev. 1:5). That's Jesus. He's the One who cares more deeply for you than any agency of the government can care for you. Jesus cares for you more than any family member can care for you. He cares for you more than any church can care for you. Jesus really cares.

Jesus and my sorrows

Jesus loved us enough to die for us, but does He love us enough to comfort us when others who are close to us die? Does He care when you've lost the dearest on earth to you? Does He care when you've lost your lifelong companion? How about when your father or mother, your son or daughter, or your best friend is gone? Does Jesus really care?

How would we know? We know because we go back to the Bible. In Luke 7 there's a touching story about a woman who had a double loss. She had earlier lost the one man she loved, her husband. She was now a widow. But she had a son who apparently lived with her and cared for her. Tragically, her son also died. While the funeral procession was making its way out of the city, the crowd encountered Jesus.

Luke tells us, "Now it happened, the day after, that He went into a city called Nain; and many of His disciples went with Him, and a large crowd. And when He came near the gate of the city, behold, a dead man was being carried out, the only son of his mother; and she was a widow. And a large crowd from the city was with her. When the Lord saw her, He had compassion on her and said to her, 'Do not weep.' Then He came and touched the open coffin, and those who carried him stood still. And He said, 'Young man, I say to you, arise.' And he who was dead sat up and began to speak. And He presented him to his mother" (vv. 11-15).

You didn't miss that, did you? You didn't miss that marvelously sympathetic heart of our Lord Jesus, the One who encountered this widow as she accompanied her son's funeral processional? "When the Lord saw her, He had compassion on her."

Does Jesus care when I've said good-by to the dearest on earth to me?

And my sad heart aches till it nearly breaks, is it aught to Him, does He see?

Well, there shouldn't be any doubt. You have your answer right here in God's Word. If you do have any doubts, when you get to heaven just ask the widow of Nain. She knows just how much Jesus cares when you lose the dearest on earth to you.

He understands your loss

What about Jesus' own loss? Remember, the Savior lost His close friend, Lazarus. When word came to Jesus that Lazarus, the brother of Mary and Martha, had died, John makes this note: "Now Jesus loved Martha and her sister and Lazarus" (John 11:5).

When Martha came to meet Jesus on the road leading into Bethany, she dropped at Jesus' feet and said, "Lord, if You had been here, my brother would not have died" (v. 21). That's our typical reaction, isn't it? When something happens, someone dear to us is taken from us, we often think, *It's the Lord's fault.*

Yet verse 33 says, "When Jesus saw her weeping, and the Jews who came with her weeping, He groaned in the spirit and was troubled."

In many respects, Mary and Martha both lashed out at the Lord Jesus, wondering why God had allowed Lazarus to be taken from them. Their neighbors came along and wept and wailed and did the same thing. When Jesus saw their grief, the Bible says He groaned in His spirit and was troubled.

Does that sound like somebody who doesn't understand you? Somebody who doesn't care when you've lost the dearest person on earth to you? I don't think so. In fact, the shortest verse of the Bible, John 11:35, records exactly how Jesus felt. It says, "Jesus wept." Right after that, the Jews noted just how much Jesus cared for this family. They said, "See how He loved him!" (v. 36).

Let me ask you, do you believe Jesus cares for you just as much as He did for Mary and Martha and Lazarus? Do you believe He cares for you just as much as He did the widow of Nain, whom He had never met before? Jesus loves you. He cares as much for you as He cares for anyone. He is just that kind of God.

Jesus and my grief

The hymn writer Daniel Whittle wrote,

Never a trial that He is not there, never a burden that He does not bear,

never a sorrow that He doth not share, moment by moment I'm under His care.

Never a heartache and never a groan, never a teardrop and never a moan,

never a danger but there on the throne, moment by moment He thinks of His own.

Maybe you're grieving the loss of someone very dear to you. Perhaps it's only been a week, a month, a year, five years. The pain never goes away, does it? I want you to know that you don't grieve alone. Jesus grieves with you, so that He can comfort you through your grieving process. He is our great High Priest. He is touched with the feelings of our infirmities. That means He is feeling exactly what you're feeling today. He hurts when you hurt. He grieves when you grieve. He loves you and He has compassion on you. He knows exactly what you're going through. He has gone through the same thing. Others may not know, but Jesus knows. And Jesus cares.

You don't have to face that dark hour alone. He is right there for you. He feels for you. He prays for you. He comforts you. Let Him do it. Pour out your heart to Him today. Let Him carry your burden.

The comfort of His care

We sometimes sing,

What a friend we have in Jesus, all our sins and griefs to bear!
What a privilege to carry everything to God in prayer!
Oh, what peace we often forfeit, oh, what needless pain we bear,
all because we do not carry everything to God in prayer.

These words are so true.

Does He care for you? Does He know what you're going through? Can you allow Him to buoy you up in His arms today? I read a story that illustrates how deeply Jesus cares and what that can mean to us. It's the story of Eric Barker.

Eric Barker was a missionary from Great Britain. He spent more than 50 years in Portugal working diligently for his Lord. Often he had to labor under adverse conditions. During the second World War, the situation became so critical in Portugal that Eric was advised to send his wife and eight children back to England for safety. His sister and her three children also were evacuated on the same ship. Although his beloved relatives were forced to leave him, he had to put them on that ship and send them away.

On the Sunday after their departure, Pastor Barker stood before his congregation and announced, "I've just received word that all my family have arrived safely home." Then Barker went on with the service as usual.

Later, the full meaning of his words became known to his people. Eric Barker had been handed a wire just before the service informing him that a submarine had torpedoed the ship and everyone on board had drowned. His wife and his eight children and his sister and her three children were all believers. For him, they had reached a more desired haven than the shores of Great Britain. He was overwhelmed with grief, but by the grace of God he managed to rise above those circumstances and finish the service.

Here's the bottom line. Jesus died for you. He paid the penalty for your sin. No one can ever care for you more than that. Jesus has over and over again proven that He cares for you.

Does Jesus care when you're all alone, when you've lost the dearest person to you? Can you go on, knowing that Jesus cares? Yes, you can. Knowing that Jesus cares will not bring your loved one back to you, but it will sustain you knowing that you do not grieve alone. He's been through it Himself. He'll help you get through it too. Jesus cares.

CONCLUSION

Oh, Yes, He Cares!

Oh, yes, He cares; I know He cares!
His heart is touched with my grief;
When the days are weary, the long nights dreary, I know my Saviour cares.

I love some of the older hymns we used to sing when I was young. We don't hear many of them anymore, and I really miss singing the message of Frank Graeff's hymn "Does Jesus Care?" It may be a while since you've sung it, too, or maybe you've never heard it before. It doesn't matter. The truth of this hymn will always be real: Jesus cares.

So whatever became of Pastor Frank Graeff? History tells us that he continued on in his ministry and became known in the Philadelphia area as the "Sunshine Minister." C. Austin Miles, a friend of Pastor Graeff, said of him in his latter years: "He is a spiritual optimist, a great friend of children; his bright sun-shining disposition attracts not only children but all with whom he comes in contact. He has a holy magnetism and a child-like faith."

From out of the depths of gloom and despair, into the sunshine of faith and joy, Pastor Graeff was led by one simple yet profound truth: "I know my Saviour cares."

Does Jesus care when your burdens press and your cares distress? Oh, yes, He cares.

Does Jesus care when your way is dark with a nameless dread and fear? I know He cares.

Does Jesus care when you've tried and failed to resist some temptation? Oh, yes, He cares.

Does Jesus care when you've said goodbye to the dearest on earth to you? His heart is touched with your grief.

When the days are weary, the long nights dreary, I know my Savior cares.

Life is not easy. The burdens can become distressingly heavy. Temptations can press in on you from every side. Dread and fear can flood your heart and wash away your peace and joy. Yet never for a moment does Jesus cease to care. Even in your darkest days when you've laid to rest one who is dearer than all others, Jesus understands and cares. He can comfort you.

Trust Him to care for you and meet your needs. He is not untouched by your trials, and in His perfect timing He will bring you out of the darkness into the light of His presence. Never forget why 1 Peter 5:7 counsels you to cast all your care upon Him. The reason? "For He cares for you."

Jesus cares!